Social Inclusion at Work

Janis Chadsey

Martin Agran and Michael Wehmeyer
Co-editors, *Innovations*

American Association on Intellectual and Developmental Disabilities

Printed in the United States of America.

Published by
American Association on Intellectual and Developmental Disabilities
444 North Capitol Street, NW
Suite 846
Washington, DC 20001-1512
www.aaidd.org

The points of view expressed herein are those of the authors and do not necessarily
represent the official policy or opinion of the American Association on Intellectual and
Developmental Disabilities. Publication does not imply endorsement by the editor,
the association, or its individual members.

ISBN 0-940898-97-7

Library of Congress Control Number: 2007906406

Table of Contents

Introduction

Successful social skills enable us to interact in ways that elicit positive responses and generally avoid negative responses.

When Jenny started her job at a local hair design studio, she was excited about her work tasks: stocking supplies, cleaning up after hair cuts, and washing customers' hair. Jenny had always been interested in the beauty industry, and Liz, her vocational and transition specialist from the high school, was excited about the job match between Jenny's career interests and her new part-time job.

As the job progressed, Liz discovered that Jenny was completing her work tasks well, but her employer was concerned about her social interactions with coworkers and customers. Specifically, Jenny was too quiet around customers and coworkers. She wasn't initiating conversations, and this made some of the customers uncomfortable.

The employer stated that the beauty industry was highly socialized, requiring employees to have good "people" skills. The employer suggested that Jenny's job be cut back to include only stocking supplies and cleaning up after hair cuts; these two tasks required fewer interactions than washing hair. But Liz knew that Jenny loved washing hair and suggested that she work with Jenny to teach her conversational initiations she could use with customers. The employer agreed to a 1-month trial period to see if Jenny could develop conversational skills that would help her succeed in her job.

The first thing Jenny and Liz did was to talk to her coworkers about the conversational topics they initiated with customers. Then Jenny watched her coworkers talking to their customers. Jenny and Liz practiced having conversations with one another, and then Jenny practiced similar conversations with her coworkers.

When Jenny initiated conversations with her coworkers outside of the practice sessions, she learned a lot about them, and they found out a lot about her. Jenny enjoyed these interactions and felt more integrated into the work setting. Jenny's success motivated her to use her new conversational skills with the customers when she washed their hair.

Jenny found that most customers really liked to talk once she asked them questions (e.g., "Have you seen any good movies lately?"). After the conversation got started, the customers often asked her questions, so the burden of the conversation did not just fall on Jenny's shoulders. Jenny's employer was pleased with Jenny's progress and told Liz that she could keep washing customers' hair.

It is clear from this example that social interactions were an important part of Jenny's job. Jenny might even have lost her job if she had not learned more effective ways to interact with her customers. Fortunately Jenny and Liz were able to work with Jenny's coworkers to determine the topics of conversations commonly used in the salon. In addition, Jenny was highly motivated and willing to practice initiating conversations with others. As a result, Jenny continued to shampoo customers' hair; she also felt more accepted by her coworkers and included in the beauty salon.

Defining Social Skills

Jenny needed to learn new social skills in order to keep her job. It is important to understand what social skills are before teaching them. Basically, successful social skills enable us to interact with others in ways that elicit positive responses and generally avoid negative responses. Let's look at four components of social skills.

What's the Reason?

First, we use social skills for specific reasons. We may want social attention from others, to meet new people, obtain information about a topic, or have specific requests fulfilled. The reasons we use social skills are varied and numerous, but it is important to remember that we always engage socially with others for a specific reason. Thus, if social skills are to be used, individuals must have a good reason for doing so, because that is why we engage in social interactions with others.

What's the Setting?

Second, our use of social skills varies with the specific social setting. For example, when we are at a party at work, we probably talk to several people, and we may use a fairly loud voice, depending upon the noise level at the party. However, in another social context, say a movie theater, our social skills would change immediately. If we talked at all, we would only whisper. If we were to use our "party" social behaviors at the movie theater, we would be asked to be quiet by other movie patrons and might be asked to leave.

What's the Context?

Third, even when we are in the same physical setting, certain social situations have an impact on the type of skills we use. For example, we would use certain types of social skills at a coworker's wedding reception located in a church hall, but would use entirely different skills in the same church if we were attending a reception for a co-worker after a funeral. These examples show that different social contexts require different social skills and also show how important it is to be able to decide which types of social skills should be used in specific social contexts.

What's the Behavior?

Finally, our social skills consist of both observable and nonobservable cognitive and affective behaviors. Certain social skills can be defined, observed, and counted. These skills might include greeting others, following directions, asking or responding to a question, telling a joke, and asking for help. Additionally, we can observe many affective, nonverbal behaviors, such as those expressing happiness, sadness, and anger.

But other social behaviors are more difficult to identify. These include being able to decode or decipher social situations to determine which social skills to use in particular situations. For example, when we meet someone for the first time, we might ask the person how she likes her work. But we also know intuitively that there are certain questions we should not ask, such as "How much do you weigh?" How do we know not to ask this question? The actual skills we use to decode or interpret social situations are difficult to define, because they have been internalized and cannot be readily observed or described. Yet those of us who are socially skilled know which type of question to ask and which not to ask across varied social situations. These skills, called social decoding skills, require us to make discriminations about social situations, then decide which of our social skills to use to fit the situation. Our use of these decoding skills contributes greatly to whether we are viewed as socially competent or incompetent.

Teaching social skills is a complex task because social skills themselves are complex. It isn't enough just to teach individuals to perform a specific observable social skill like greeting others upon arrival at work. We also need to explain why they would want to greet others; under which social situations they should greet; and when, with whom, and how they should greet. The nature of social skills requires that we teach employees a specific skill, as well as how to discriminate under which circumstances the skill should be used.

The Purpose of This Book

This book, intended for secondary teachers, transitional and vocational specialists, job coaches, and other service providers, illustrates how to socially integrate people with disabilities into employment settings. This is based on the premise that being included in the social group increases job security and quality-of-life outcomes.

> Of 1,243 indicators of quality of life, the dimension with the greatest number of indicators was social relationships.
>
> —Hughes, Hwang, Kim, Eisenman, & Killian (1995)

Chapter 2 discusses the importance of social interactions in work settings and provides examples of social interactions that may occur in just about every job. In addition, Chapter 2 describes social skills important for job retention and job satisfaction. Finally, there is a list of social behaviors valued by employers.

Chapter 3 identifies assessment measures to determine if someone is included socially in a work setting. Before we design intervention strategies, we first need to know what kinds of behaviors and results we are trying to achieve.

Strategies to assess the specific social skills of employees with disabilities are discussed.

Chapters 4 and 5 present intervention strategies to support the inclusion of an individual in an employment setting. Essentially there are two groups of intervention strategies: The first group comprises natural support strategies to change the social behavior of coworkers as well as other aspects of the work setting. The second group is designed to change the social behavior of the person with disabilities. Chapter 6 gives guidelines for determining which strategies to use.

Chapter 7 presents a detailed case study of Mara, which shows the steps used to help Mara become a social member of a coworker group at a local fitness center.

Chapter 8 summarizes the main points of the book.

Social Skills in Employment Settings

A person with competent social skills is more likely to get and keep a job than someone without them.

Social Interactions at Work

Frequency of Interactions

It would be difficult to find any job where social interactions did not occur. One might think that writers or painters would have little need for social interactions with others, but artists and writers have to work with agents, editors, and the public in promoting their products. Having said that, some jobs may require fewer social interactions than others, an important point to consider, especially when we think about making job matches for people with disabilities.

When making a job match, we need to consider both job-task and social-task matches. If a person with a disability enjoys the specific work tasks but is not happy with the social aspects of a job, the job match will not be ideal. In such a case, the social desires and skills of the individual may not match the social characteristics of the job. If a person is highly social, jobs with highly social work-cultures should be considered as potential matches. Similarly if a person does not enjoy interacting with others and prefers to work primarily alone, jobs that do not rely on social interactions should be considered as potential matches.

Because social interactions occur in nearly every job, it is important to consider their importance and frequency when making job matches. Without doing so, job failure may occur.

Types of Relationships

When people display competent social interactions, they can form social relationships with others. Several types of social relationships can occur in work settings: work acquaintances, work friends, and social friends. Work acquaintances are superficial relationships mostly oriented around work tasks. Generally, we would have neutral feelings about our work acquaintances. Work friends are individuals we feel closer to than acquaintances. We might share a lot of personal information with them, but we probably would not see them outside of work. Our closest relationships are with our social friends. These are individuals with whom we would share our innermost thoughts and feelings; we'd probably spend time with them outside of work.

In the workplace, people with disabilities often have only work acquaintances or work friends, not social friends. It isn't necessary to have all three types of relationships at work. But if we do not get along well with others at work, and if we do not even have work acquaintances, we may be at risk of losing our jobs and feeling lonely, sad, or resentful.

Job Retention and Satisfaction

A person with competent social skills is more likely to get and keep a job than someone without them. In fact, considerable evidence suggests that workers with disabilities are more likely to lose their jobs because of inappropriate social behavior than because of difficulties in performing their job tasks.

Consider the case of Jane, who was hired as a hotel maid. Each day she had a quota of rooms to clean. One day she was behind schedule and time was running short. She came to her last room and found a "Do Not Disturb" sign on the door. Jane was upset that she could not clean this particular room. She knocked on the door and said, "Get your butt out of bed!" Unfortunately Jane lost her job because of this inappropriate social behavior, even though she was competent at cleaning rooms.

Although anyone can lose a job because of inappropriate social behaviors, people with disabilities might have more problems because of difficulties with receptive and expressive language skills. Although people can lose jobs for social reasons related to theft and aggression, employees can also lose their jobs for more subtle social problems, such as talking too much, complaining about job duties, or disturbing other employees (or in Jane's case, above, disturbing customers).

Competent social skills help us keep our jobs and may have a positive impact on our job satisfaction. Employees with appropriate social skills are likely to form social relationships, which can contribute to a positive quality of life. Having positive social relationships has been associated with lower levels of stress and higher levels of happiness. In interviews about factors that contribute to a high quality of life, people, including those with disabilities, talk about friends and close social relationships.

We, of course, form social relationships in many settings, such as schools, neighborhoods, and clubs, but social relationships may be particularly important at work. Full-time employees spend at least 8 hours a day at their jobs. This provides frequent opportunities for workers to get to know one another. In addition, the work context provides workers with common experiences, pressures, concerns, and vocabulary, and a culture to create a common basis for forming relationships. Positive social relationships are associated with greater job satisfaction.

> For those employed, work settings are frequently the second most important social unit after the immediate family context.
>
> —Stewart (1995)

Employers Value Social Skills

Over the years, employers have been asked to identify the types of social skills important in the workplace. Desirable social skills fall into two categories, those directly related to work duties and those not related to work duties. Both types of interactions are important in work settings, but for different reasons.

Work-related social skills include behaviors such as following directions, requesting assistance, sharing work information, and responding to criticism. Employers tend to value work-related social skills because they directly contribute to task completion.

Non-work-related social skills might include behaviors such as teasing and joking, sharing information about sports, or asking about a coworker's family. These social skills are important for getting along with coworkers and fitting into the work setting but do not relate directly to productivity. Non-work-related social skills help coworkers discover common interests and share intimate details and thus contribute to the development of social relationships.

Table 1 lists some of the observed work-related and non-work-related social skills employers consider important in work settings. Note that not all of these skills are important in all work settings.

As you work with individuals with disabilities, you'll want to determine which types of social skills particular employers value. Employers could be interviewed personally. Or you might send employers a short survey that includes the skills listed in Table 1, asking them to rate the importance of each skill to the job as (a) critical, (b) important, (c) useful, or (d) not necessary. Either method would provide information about the specific social skills employers see as important.

Table 1

Valued Social Behaviors in Employment Settings

- Following directions
- Reciting full name on request
- Asking for assistance
- Responding to criticism
- Getting information before starting a job
- Offering to help coworkers
- Listening without interrupting
- Expressing appreciation
- Teasing and joking
- Using social amenities (e.g., thank you)
- Providing information about a job
- Asking questions
- Conversing with others
- Greeting others

It might also be helpful to interview and/or observe coworkers, because employers might not be aware of the non-work-related social skills important on the job. In interviews, you might ask coworkers what types of social skills they value on the job. Or you might observe coworkers interacting to see what they talk about and what kind of social skills they use. It seems that workers talk to coworkers with disabilities about work-related topics more than about non-work-related topics. Identifying non-work-related social skills can be useful for helping an employee with disabilities to become socially included in work settings.

Summary

Although social interactions occur in every job, they may be more important for some jobs (e.g., food service) than for others (e.g., manufacturing). It is important that the social aspects of the job match the social skills and interests of the person looking for a job. Job retention and job satisfaction are likely to increase if a good social match is made, if one has developed some type of social relationship on the job (e.g., work acquaintance, work friend, social friend), and if one performs various valued and observed social behaviors (e.g., following directions, listening without interrupting, offering to help others) that employers have identified as important.

Assessing Social Inclusion in Employment Settings

*Unfortunately there is
not a single question to ask or
a single test to give that will tell
if someone is socially included.*

In this chapter, two questions are addressed regarding social inclusion assessment. What behaviors and perceptions indicate whether social inclusion is occurring in an employment setting? What strategies can be used to assess these behaviors and perceptions?

Social Inclusion: Behaviors and Perceptions

How do we know if someone is socially included on the job? This is a complex question to answer. Unfortunately there is not a single question to ask or a single test to give that will tell if someone is socially included. Because social inclusion is complex, one needs to assess at least four aspects to determine whether it has been achieved: (a) social participation, (b) social acceptance by coworkers, (c) feelings and perceptions of the individual with disabilities, and (d) appropriate social skills.

Social Participation

Social participation refers to the type, scope, and frequency of participation in social activities at work. All workers engage in some type of social activity in their jobs. The assessment task is to determine which social activities occur in particular work settings and whether the individual with a disability is participating in these social activities.

Social Activities

Social activities take place in specific social contexts where interactions are likely to occur. How do we figure out which social activities occur at particular work sites? Many social activities can be observed, or one can ask employers and/or coworkers about typical work-site social activities.

Some social activities seem to be generic to every work site (Table 2), for example, interacting with others "during arrival." When employees arrive at work and first see other employees, they frequently talk. They might greet each other and ask how the other is doing, talk about the weather, mention a television show they watched the night before, or discuss the work that needs to

be accomplished that day. Though brief, the social interchanges that occur "during arrival at work" may be important to the day's start-up and may serve as an initial social bond for coworkers.

To determine if an employee with a disability is participating in the social activity of "arrival at work," we need to know:

1. When does "arrival at work" occur?

2. Where do employees gather when they first arrive at work?

3. What do employees generally talk about when they arrive at work?

4. Is the employee with a disability participating in the "arrival at work" social activity? Is the employee there at the right time and place, and is the employee included in the conversations?

Table 2 lists other work-setting social activities. Employees are likely to interact with one another during scheduled break times and during lunch. They also may socially interact at the completion of a job task, especially if the task is completed by an established team or more informally by two or more people working in close proximity. Employees may talk about the completed tasks or about nonwork topics. In many work settings, it is permissible to interact while working; workers just need to make certain that their social interactions do not interfere with getting the job done.

Other social activities may occur in work settings, but with less frequency and regularity than those discussed above. Participation in some infrequent social activities, such as company-sponsored birthday parties, picnics, or holiday parties, may still be critical to social inclusion. Still other social activities that occur outside the work setting may also contribute toward social inclusion. For example, coworkers may gather

---

Table 2

Possible Positive Social Participation Behaviors

- Participating socially during arrival at work

- Participating socially during breaks

- Participating socially during lunch

- Participating socially during the completion of work tasks

- Participating socially during company-sponsored events (e.g., birthday parties, holiday gatherings)

- Participating socially after work (e.g., going to a coworker's house for dinner)

---

once a week to eat lunch at a nearby restaurant or get together for a Friday night drink at a local bar. Some coworkers may occasionally gather for potluck suppers held at various homes.

Workplace Culture

To assess social activities, especially those that do not occur regularly or frequently, it's important to have some knowledge of the culture of the workplace. What do we mean by workplace culture? The term refers to the shared meanings and values that influence how people interact with one another and conduct their business at the workplace. The culture of a particular workplace may not always be obvious and may take some time to figure out. But to "fit in," an employee needs to understand the culture of a work setting.

For example, one hotel in a small Midwestern town had an unspoken rule that when workers arrived in the morning, they took turns bringing a treat for the owner's ever-present dog. No one told new hires that they had to participate in this social activity, but all eventually figured out that this was expected behavior if they wanted to fit in.

An understanding of the work culture will help teachers, job coaches, and other service providers identify the social activities important for social participation. Once these are specified, it can be determined when they occur, what people talk about, and if the worker with disabilities is socially participating in the activities. (For more information about work cultures, see the section on Natural Support Strategies.)

> Employees who "fit in" to their work cultures are more likely to be accepted by their coworkers and judged as being successful by their employers.
> —Wayne & Lidden (1995)

Social Acceptance by Coworkers

A second aspect to assess is how well a worker is socially accepted by other coworkers. Information can be obtained in various ways. Certainly we could observe coworkers interacting with a worker, and we could note if the interactions seemed positive, neutral, or negative. This type of information gives us some insight about the type of affect associated with interactions between coworkers with and without disabilities. But it may be difficult to assess a person's level and type of acceptance simply by noting the affect associated with social interactions. One person might display a positive affect when interacting with someone and still not like that person very much. Or a co-

---

Table 3

Possible Social Acceptance Behaviors

Coworkers indicate they like to:

- Work with the person
- Eat lunch with the person
- Take breaks with the person
- See the person after work
- Attend company social events with the person
- Advocate for the person
- Consider the person to be an acquaintance
- Consider the person to be a work friend
- Consider the person to be a social friend

worker might interact neutrally but still be willing to advocate for or support the person.

The best way to gather information is by asking coworkers how they feel about the individual with a disability. This assumes that coworkers will respond honestly to questions asked (tell us how they honestly feel and not what they think we want them to say).

Specific questions can help determine an employee's level of acceptance (Table 3). For example, we could assess whether coworkers like to work with the individual with disabilities, like to eat lunch or take breaks with the person, see the person after work, or attend company social events with him or her. We could also determine if coworkers consider the person to be an acquaintance, a work friend, or a social friend. The answers to these types of questions tell us about the type and depth of acceptance experienced by a particular person.

Feelings and Perceptions

To further assess social inclusion at work, we need to consider the feelings and perceptions of individuals with disabilities. Table 4 gives categories to help you formulate questions to ask; many of the potential questions resemble those we might ask coworkers. For example, we might ask the employees with disabilities if they like to work with their coworkers, eat lunch and take breaks with them, attend company social events, and see coworkers after work. We might also ask if an individual has acquaintances, work friends, and social friends. Additionally, we might ask if the worker is happy or lonely at work. Finally, it might be useful to see if the worker wishes he had more (or fewer) interactions with coworkers or more or fewer friends at work.

Again, this information is best obtained from employees with disabilities, but gathering this type of information may be problematic if employees have difficulty understanding the questions being asked or do not have reliable or conventional forms of expression. Observing interactions between employees and coworkers and determining if employees with disabilities display positive, neutral, or negative affects during these interactions may be instructive, but, again, direct observations of interactions may not always indicate the true feelings of individuals.

Table 4

Possible Positive Feelings and Perceptions

Individuals with disabilities indicate they like to:

- Work with the coworkers

- Eat lunch with the coworkers

- Take breaks with the coworkers

- See the coworkers after work

- Attend company social events with the coworkers

- Advocate for the coworkers

- Consider one or more coworkers to be acquaintances

- Consider one or more coworkers to be work friends

- Consider one or more coworkers to be social friends

- Express happiness with their social situation at work

Appropriate Social Skills

The last aspect to assess is the social skills of the employee with disabilities. Essentially we want to determine if the employee uses appropriate social skills in social interactions with coworkers and employers. Social skills are deemed appropriate if the responses of others are positive or neutral and not negative and if there is some degree of reciprocity or exchange.

It is difficult to pinpoint specific appropriate social skills to assess because each work setting requires its own set of social skills. Having said that, the social skills listed in Table 1 are easily observed and valued in most work settings. You might want to measure these among others you identify.

Be sure to assess the social skills actually used and valued in each specific work setting and any other social skills that are critical to the well-being of the employee. For example, it may be important to assess the self-determination skills of an employee. If an employee cannot advocate for herself, be involved in setting her own goals, and be a persistent problem-solver, others may take advantage. Poor self-determination skills may also influence the feelings and perceptions of the individual; that is, an employee may not be happy in a work setting if she feels she has no choice or control in that setting.

> Historically students with disabilities were passive and inactive in planning their lives and making decisions; now, they must be self-determined and actively involved in this process.
>
> —Wehmeyer (1998)

When assessing social skills, it is important to distinguish between work-related and non-work-related social skills. For example, an employee may be able to ask work-related questions (e.g., Where is the soap?), but may not be able to ask non-work-related questions (e.g., What did you do over the weekend?). By pinpointing the specific social skill that the person is lacking (e.g., asking questions) and noting that the lack is exhibited only during non-work-related interactions, the assessment information helps teachers, job coaches, and other service providers hone an intervention strategy.

Being socially adept involves more than being able to exhibit or display appropriate social skills. It is also knowing how to interpret and discriminate social situations and cues from others. This means that individuals know when, how, and with whom to interact in a socially appropriate manner.

For example, when Pete goes out for a drink with his coworkers after work, he is very good at asking for assistance in a bar. If he spills a drink, he knows how to approach a stranger (e.g., bartender) and ask for a cloth to wipe the spill. Because bars are often very noisy, Pete knows to speak in a loud voice. However, Pete would be judged as exhibiting inappropriate social skills if he did the same thing (i.e., asked a stranger for help in a very loud voice) in a public library. Pete would be judged as exhibiting inappropriate social skills, not because of being unable to request assistance, but because of asking the wrong person for assistance in the wrong manner for the particular social context (i.e., the library).

Here are four questions to ask when assessing the use of appropriate social skills:

1. Does the individual exhibit valued social skills (e.g., those identified as important by key stakeholders such as employers or coworkers)?

2. Are the social skills work-related or non-work-related?

3. When the social skills are performed, do they result in positive, neutral, or negative responses from others?

4. Are the social skills performed with the right person, at the right time, and in the right place or situation?

Summary

Four assessments should be completed to determine if an employee with a disability is being socially included in a work setting.

First, one needs to assess whether the employee is participating in social activities at work. Determine which social activities occur in the work setting and whether the employee with a disability is actively involved in them.

Second, one needs to know if the employee is accepted by coworkers. This requires understanding the nature and extent of acceptance experienced by the employee.

Third, the feelings and perceptions of the employee with a disability must be assessed. One should understand how employees with disabilities feel about their social relationships with others and their overall social situation at work.

The fourth assessment considers whether the employee is exhibiting social skills appropriate for the particular work culture.

To summarize, the assessment of social inclusion is a complex yet valuable undertaking. At least four aspects should be measured to determine if someone is socially included in his or her work setting. If only one of these areas was assessed, one would not have a true picture of social inclusion. In the next section, we discuss assessment strategies.

Assessment Strategies

There are four strategies for assessing social inclusion: (a) direct observation, (b) sociometrics, (c) rating scales, and (d) role plays. Much has been written about these assessment strategies, because all of them have been used to assess other types of behavior (e.g., math skills). Because there is not enough space here to describe thoroughly each procedure, consult other sources and books on assessment for an in-depth treatment. In this section, the strategies are discussed in relation to their usefulness for assessing social inclusion.

Direct Observation

Direct observation can be used to assess all four aspects of social inclusion. Here a person watches what is going on and records what is seen and heard. An individual may record what is occurring in the observed interaction (e.g., noting with whom the employee is interacting, where they are interacting, and the topics of their interaction). Or an observer may count how often a particular behavior occurs (e.g., the number of times the employee initiates a work-related topic while completing work tasks). It also might be important to record the duration of an interaction (i.e., how long it lasts), such as an interaction between two coworkers during lunch.

Social Participation

Direct observation is a useful strategy for determining what social activities take place in a particular work setting. An observer can watch the workers to see when and where they interact (e.g., in the coffee room at 10:00 a.m.). One can also record what the workers talk about. After determining which social activities occur in a work site, one can also observe whether employees with disabilities are physically present in the activity and are participating socially in some manner (e.g., initiating conversations or responding to others' initiations).

Social Acceptance

Direct observation is probably not the best strategy for measuring the social acceptance by coworkers of the employee with a disability, because although coworkers may behave one way (e.g., smile when in the company of an employee with a disability), they may actually feel another way (e.g., don't really like the employee). Having said that, direct observation may be your best alternative if it is inappropriate or uncomfortable to ask coworkers directly how they feel about the individual. One can observe how coworkers interact with the employee and evaluate the quality of the interactions, noting if they are positive, neutral, or negative.

Feelings and Perceptions

Similar comments can be made about using direct observation to assess the feelings and perceptions of employees with disabilities. One can watch employees with disabilities interact with their coworkers and judge whether their interactions are positive, neutral, or negative. Again, this may not be the best strategy; how employees behave may not really be how they feel. Nevertheless, direct observation may provide useful information, particularly if employees with disabilities have difficulty understanding the language used to ask questions (e.g., Do you feel lonely at work?), or if employees have difficulty expressing themselves in a conventional manner (i.e., through verbal or augmentative means).

Social Skills

One may also directly observe and record an employee's use of social skills, judging their appropriateness for the particular work setting. For example, you might observe an employee during break and count the number of times the employee starts a conversation (or responds to another's comments) and the length of time other coworkers spend in conversations with the employee. One can assess the greeting skills of an employee when he arrives at work and how the employee responds to work requests from the employer. This is a useful strategy for assessing the use of numerous social skills, because one can actually observe whether they are occurring and make informed judgments about their appropriateness for specific work cultures.

Disadvantages and Advantages

Although direct observation can be used to measure all four aspects of social inclusion, there are disadvantages to consider. First, it is a time-consuming assessment strategy, in that it requires teachers, job coaches, or other service providers to curtail other activities and observe the employee.

Second, direct observation may be intrusive and alter the social behaviors observed. In some work cultures, it may not be appropriate to observe the social behavior of others. The presence of an observer may make some employers, coworkers, and customers uncomfortable, consequently, they may not act naturally. (Note: It is possible to observe in a covert manner. After a while people get used to being observed, then behave as they normally would if they were not being observed.)

The third disadvantage is that direct observation may not prove to be useful for assessing behaviors that occur infrequently; the scheduled observation times may not coincide with the occurrence of the social behavior of interest.

Even so, there are advantages of using direct observation as an assessment strategy. It is a measure of overt behavior, giving us the best under-

Figure 1
Coworker Rating Scale

Directions: Below is a list of the people you work with. For each person, please assign a number from 1 to 9 to show how you feel about working with the person, eating lunch or taking breaks with the person, talking with the person during work, and doing things with the person away from work. Giving someone a "1" means you like to do things with him or her a lot. A "9" means you don't like to do things with the person. A 10 means you don't have an opinion about the person. No one will know your ratings; they are confidential.

Rate using these numbers:

Like a Lot				Neutral				Don't Like
1	2	3	4	5	6	7	8	9

10 – No Opinion

Coworkers	Work With the Person	Eat Lunch or Take Breaks With the Person	Talk With the Person During Work	Do Things With the Person Outside Work
1.				
2.				
3.				
4.				
5.				
6.				
7.				
8.				
9.				
10.				

standing of social behavior because it enables us to see what happens before, during, and after the occurrence of social behaviors.

Sociometrics

Sociometrics, which provides information about an individual's social status and relationships with others, has been used primarily in school settings, but it can also be useful in employment settings. Using this approach, individuals (coworkers, in this case) are asked to respond to items on a written questionnaire that probes their feelings and perceptions about other people in their work environment.

Two Rating Types

There are two types of sociometric strategies: nomination and rating.

Using the nomination strategy, you might ask coworkers to name two people in the work setting with whom they like to work, eat lunch, see outside the work setting, and whom they consider to be their friends. You might ask coworkers to name two people with whom they do not like to do these things.

Using the sociometric rating strategy, you might provide coworkers with a questionnaire that lists everyone with whom they work and ask them to circle a number on a scale (e.g., from 1 to 9) that indicates how much they like to work with the person, consider the person to be a friend, take breaks with him or her, and so on. The scale is anchored by words that describe different feelings. For example, circling 1 indicates that coworkers do not like to do things with the particular person they are rating, whereas circling 9 indicates that they really like to do things with the person they are rating. Figure 1 illustrates a sociometric rating scale that has been used in employment settings.

Measuring Acceptance and Feelings

Sociometrics is helpful for measuring how people in the work setting feel about each other. Teachers, job coaches, and other service providers can use this strategy to determine if employees with disabilities are accepted or are having relational problems with coworkers. Similarly the strategy can be used to gather information from employees with disabilities about their feelings and perceptions of their coworkers. The strategy can also provide information about the status of coworkers; it might be useful to see who the popular or well-liked coworkers are in order to enlist their help in devising inclusion strategies.

Both the nomination and rating strategies can be tailored to provide the specific information needed by service providers. Sociometric strategies can be individualized to specific work sites and coworkers. As a starting point, the sociometric forms can include some of the items listed in Tables 3 and 4.

Disadvantages and Advantages

There are several disadvantages of the sociometric assessment strategy. First, the results will not provide information about specific social skills that might need to be changed to promote better social relationships; the information simply indicates how coworkers in the setting feel about the people with whom they work.

Second, coworkers may feel uncomfortable about filling out such a form about colleagues. If this assessment strategy disrupts the work culture or seems too unusual, it probably should not be used.

Third, it would be difficult to gather this type of information if coworkers, or the employees with disabilities, cannot read. To address this dilemma, you might read the items to coworkers and have them circle or point to a series of three faces that correspond to particular feelings:

Figure 2

Rating Scale for Nonreaders: Feelings

Positive Feelings   Neutral Feelings   Negative Feelings

positive, neutral, or negative (Figure 2). Coworkers can be interviewed about their feelings and perceptions, but they might not express their true feelings; they might respond as they think the interviewer wants them to. Also, they may express an immediate feeling that does not accurately reflect their typical feeling about the individual (e.g., if they are interviewed after having a disagreement).

Nonetheless, sociometric assessment is the best strategy for providing information about friendship patterns and coworker status in work settings. Additionally, it may be of value to see how this information compares to any observational data collected. If there is agreement between what was observed and what was expressed, each strategy confirms the other. If there is a discrepancy, this would indicate that how coworkers behave toward a person with a disability may not reveal true feelings.

Rating Scales

The use of rating scales is similar to sociometric assessments. Both methods typically use questionnaires that consist of items rated on a particular dimension (e.g., frequency of behavior). Both methods can be tailored to provide the information needed from an individual employment setting, because all items can be individualized. Where the scales differ is in their purpose:

> Sociometric scales provide information about relationships (e.g., friendships) and status among the coworkers in the setting; rating scales provide information about specific social behaviors and skills.

Rating Participation and Skills

Rating scales can be used to assess two aspects of social inclusion: social participation and appropriate social skills.

For example, coworkers could be asked to list all the social activities and settings they frequent. Or they could be given a list of social activities such as those in Table 2 and asked to indicate on a scale of 1 (not very often) to 5 (every day) how frequently they participate. Such a rating scale could provide useful knowledge about popular social activities in work settings. Social participation could also be assessed by having coworkers or employers rate the frequency with which the employee with disabilities participates in the social activities at work. Again, this information could be rated on a scale of 1 (does not participate very often) to 5 (participates every day).

Table 5

Employer Rating Scale

Directions: Make a checkmark in the column that indicates how frequently the social skill is performed.

Work- and Non-Work-Related Social Skills	Always Does Does This Skill	Sometimes Does This Skill	Rarely Does This Skill
Follows directions			
Recites full name on request			
Asks for assistance			
Responds to criticism			
Gets information before starting a job			
Offers to help coworkers			
Listens without interrupting			
Expresses appreciation			

Rating scales can also be used to assess the social skills used by the employee with disabilities. Social skills can be listed on a questionnaire, and coworkers and even the employer can be asked whether the employee uses these skills appropriately. Table 5 is an example.

Rating scales can also be used to identify the social skills most important in a particular work setting. For example, employers can be provided with a list of social skills and asked to rate them as "not important" (e.g., by circling 1) to "very important" (e.g., by circling 5).

Rating scales can be used to assess a wide range of behaviors and skills; however, the disadvantages are that they may offer only global ratings of behavior, and there is a potential for rater bias. Similar to sociometrics, rating scales may be problematic if the individuals doing the ratings have poor literacy skills.

Role Plays

The fourth assessment strategy, role play, is useful for assessing appropriate social skills. Employees with disabilities can be asked to demonstrate particular social skills by performing or role playing the skill in a simulated social context. For example, employees with disabilities might be asked to show how they greet people when they arrive at work.

Table 6

Strategies for Assessing Social Inclusion

Strategy	Applicable to Assess	Advantages	Disadvantages
Direct Observation	• Social participation • Social acceptance by coworkers • Feelings and perceptions of individuals with disabilities • Appropriate social skills	• Can be used to measure all four social inclusion outcomes • Provides an objective measure • Enables observer to see what happens before and after a social behavior or interaction occurs	• Is time consuming • Is intrusive • Is not the most accurate for assessing perceptions and feelings • Is not useful for low-incidence behavior
Sociometrics	• Social acceptance by coworkers • Feelings and perceptions of individual with disabilities	• Provides information on social status • Provides information on relationship with others • Can individualize items to measure those of interest	• Does not provide information on specific social skills that might need to be changed • Might make coworkers filling it out feel uncomfortable • Is difficult to use with nonreaders
Rating Scales	• Social participation • Appropriate social skills	• Provides information on wide range of social behaviors and skills • May allow items to be individualized	• Offers only global ratings • Introduces potential for rater bias
Role Plays	• Appropriate social skills	• Can design unlimited types of social scenarios that assess many social behaviors • Can be used to assess low-incident social behaviors • Assesses skills in "safe" environment	• May not be valid

With this assessment strategy, teachers, job coaches, and other service providers design a series of role plays that typically consist of actual social scenarios found to exist in the employment setting. For example, one role play might assess how an employee responds to criticism from an employer. The person doing the assessment describes the social scenario to the employee and observes the employee's response.

The specific scenario might be: "Let's say that part of your job is to lock the door to the office every night when you leave. Last night you forgot to do this. The employer says to you, 'John, you forgot to lock the office last night; this does not make me happy. It is important that you remember to lock the office, because there are important materials in there. I expect that you will not make this mistake again.' "

After presenting the social scenario to the employee, you ask the employee how he or she would respond to the employer. The employee's response would indicate how the employee might react to criticism from an employer.

There are several advantages to using role plays to assess social skills. First, the number and type of social scenarios that can be designed are unlimited; however, all social scenarios need to be ones that actually exist in the employment setting.

Second, the social scenarios can depict social situations that may not occur very often but may be crucial to being included in the work setting.

Third, you can assess the employee's behavior in a safe environment. Usually role play assessments are conducted outside of work hours, and often in settings other than the work setting; if the employee has trouble exhibiting an appropriate social skill, the skill assessment (role play) will have no negative impact.

Like the other assessment methods, role playing has disadvantages, primarily that the assessments may not be totally valid; that is, an employee may be able to demonstrate the use of an appropriate social skill during a role play, but may not be able to demonstrate the same skill in a work setting. To offset this disadvantage, direct observation methods can be used to confirm whether the social skill demonstrated during the role play is also used in the work setting.

Summary

Four types of strategies can be used to assess social inclusion: direct observation, sociometrics, rating scales, and role plays. Table 6 presents information about these strategies: What social inclusion aspects do they assess? What are the advantages and disadvantages of each strategy? Unfortunately there is not one best strategy for assessing social inclusion. Instead, there are advantages to using multiple strategies, thereby providing greater insight about social interactions and coworker and employee perceptions.

Changing the Social Context and Environment

The culture of the work setting helps dictate what interventions should be tried.

Two types of intervention strategies can be used to facilitate social inclusion: natural support strategies and social skill training strategies. In this chapter we discuss natural support intervention strategies.

To facilitate the social inclusion of employees with disabilities, first consider using natural support strategies. These strategies are especially useful if the employee has trouble learning new social skills, if the employee is not motivated to work on social skills, or if social inclusion is likely to result from changes in people in the work setting rather than from changes in the social skills of the employee with a disability.

Natural Support Strategies

Typically, when we think of facilitating the social inclusion of employees with disabilities, we think about implementing an intervention to change the employee's social skills. However, other changes in the work setting may be called for. Strategies to make these modifications are called natural support strategies.

Natural support strategies are services or resources that already exist in a work setting. For example, coworkers can be thought of as a natural support resource. In many work settings, coworkers help to facilitate the inclusion of new coworkers. In fact, when most people start a new job, they are trained (and sometimes befriended) by a coworker who "shows them the ropes." It is quite possible that when an employee with a disability is hired, a coworker might be assigned to show him the job duties and general day-to-day functioning of the job. This naturally occurring event may help to promote the inclusion of an employee with a disability without the job coach, teacher, or other service provider designing specific inclusion interventions.

There are other types of natural support strategies to promote social inclusion. For example, there may be ways to modify a work schedule or work duties so the employee with the disability has more opportunities to interact with other coworkers. These types of strategies involve changing aspects of the environment.

Finally, there may be certain characteristics associated with jobs, such as the leadership style of the boss or the informality of the work setting, that promote inclusion on their own. If you look for work settings with some of these characteristics, and if these settings match the needs and desires of the employee with the disabilities, you may not need other intervention strategies.

Before discussing in more depth specific types of natural support strategies, I will summarize aspects of work cultures, because it is the culture of the work setting that helps to dictate what interventions should be tried.

Culture of Work Settings

Every work setting is made up of people and traditions that influence the day-to-day functioning of the setting. People who are included in the work culture know the "rules" and meet the expectations by sharing values, traditions, and assumptions.

Long-Standing Customs

Some of the rules that define a work culture are not written down but are apparent through observation or interviews. Below is an example of a cultural custom observed at Kennedy High School. This custom isn't written down anywhere at the school, but everyone who is included in the culture knows that it exists.

At Kennedy High School, each teacher always sits in a specific chair in the teacher's lounge. In fact, no one would ever think of sitting in someone else's chair. How did this custom start? Over time the teachers began to sit in the same chairs, and the chairs became individualized. If a new person came into the lounge and sat in someone else's chair, that person would be committing an inappropriate social act without even knowing it! Certainly a person would not be fired for sitting in the wrong chair in the teacher's lounge, but a person might experience some type of social ostracism from the other teachers.

The example of the chairs in the teacher's lounge shows how a simple way of behaving can eventually become a strictly observed custom. Many other examples of cultural rules might not be in writing but nevertheless are important for someone being socially included in a work setting. For example, some offices always celebrate people's birthdays by going out for a drink on a Friday night. It might be the expectation that everyone should go. Although acceptable to miss an occasional Friday night, a number of absences might be perceived as a violation of the cultural norms at the workplace. No one would be fired for not attending the Friday night celebration, but lack of attendance might negatively influence social inclusion.

Managerial Priorities

The style and priorities of management also influence some cultural norms. Here is an example: A prominent engineering company in a small Midwestern town is housed in a conservative but attractively designed building, faced with red brick. Inside, customers see plaques showing the number of years various employees have worked for the firm as well as plaques representing company awards. After the plaques the most prominent focal point is a huge wooden desk that is so high that from the door you can see only the heads of the receptionists—who, when visitors enter, look up and greet them with a smile. The receptionists are very well groomed and wear dresses, suits, and other tailored clothes. Other employees are similarly dressed.

Without even talking to anyone who works in this building, we already understand the culture of this work setting; it is formal. We can already tell how we are going to have to behave and what kinds of clothes we are expected to wear. If we were looking for jobs for employees with disabilities and were considering this engineering firm, we would know that we would have to find someone who would want to work in a formal setting.

Work Culture and Inclusion

Some work settings have more distinct cultures than others. It is important to understand different work cultures because they can influence someone's social inclusion. In addition, they can influence completion of work tasks, especially when work is done jointly with other people. This means that any intervention to socially include an employee with a disability should be designed to fit in with the culture. An intervention that seemed odd or unusual for the work setting probably would not be very successful. Also, any planned intervention involving coworkers or other natural supports should take into consideration the coworkers' comfort level; otherwise you risk violating cultural norms.

Hagner (2000) believes that 31 different elements of a work culture need to be assessed to gain an understanding of the culture of a particular employment setting.

For these reasons, it is important to learn something about the workplace culture before designing interventions that use natural support strategies, or even before designing interventions to teach social skills to employees with disabilities.

To assess a work culture, observe or talk to other people about workplace factors. Pay attention to the clothes people wear, how they decorate their personal space, if they seem to help each other out, and where they hang out and talk. Try to find out if the business sponsors certain social activities (e.g., holiday parties, birthday parties) and if there are specific social rituals in which everyone takes part (e.g., taking turns filling up a candy jar). Also observe the general social interaction style used by coworkers, noting whether it is formal or informal. Do people talk about topics other than work tasks? Do they tease and joke? These observations will provide important information about the work culture of a particular setting.

Using Natural Supports to Make Workplace Matches

The easiest and best way to ensure someone's social inclusion in a work setting is to make a good job match. Although it is important to consider whether prospective employees will like and be able to do the tasks associated with the job, it is also important to consider whether employees have good social matches.

Minimal Intervention

When trying to make a good social match on the job for an employee, the first course of action is to rely on the supports, services, and resources that already exist naturally in the work setting. If you're able to make a good job match, it is possible that you won't have to design any other type of social intervention; an employee will just "naturally" fit in by virtue of the resources and supports in the work setting.

Or you may have to design some relatively minor intervention to assist an employee's adjustment. But, again, if the job match is a good one, the intervention may not take much planning or effort.

Only when one has to design an intrusive intervention does one realize that one has not made a good job match. If employees start a new job and immediately have trouble getting along with coworkers, you have not made a successful social match. This situation does not mean that employees will be fired or should quit, but it may take more intervention to assist employees in becoming socially included.

> The type of support selected for an employee should be secondary to a good job match.
>
> —Mank, Cioffi, & Yovanoff (2000)

Strategies to Facilitate Matches

What is the best way to make a good social match between a person and a job?

First, find out about the social goals of the employee by assessing her perceptions and feelings (Table 4). If you know that the individual is interested in meeting new people and making new friends, look for a job that offers this opportunity.

Table 7

Strategies for Making Personal and Inclusive Job Matches

1. Consider the individual's social goals. Does the person want to meet new people and develop new social relationships? If yes, look for a job where this can occur.

2. Consider the individual's social skills. Is this person highly social? Or is the person happier where interaction is not an important part of the job task?

3. Look for jobs where all employees work the same shift and at the same time.

4. Look for jobs where the employer or supervisor uses an informal style of management and encourages employees to work as a team.

5. Look for jobs where the employer or supervisor often talks to coworkers about topics not related to work.

6. Look for jobs where there are designated areas for coworkers to interact with one another.

7. Look for jobs where coworkers share social activities away from the work setting.

If you have assessed appropriate social skills (Table 1), you will know something about the social "personality" of the employee. If the employee is sociable and likes to interact with others, you'll want to look for a job situation that offers social opportunities. If the individual does not like to interact with others and prefers more solitary activities, look for a work environment that is not highly social.

Other features of work settings can help workers with disabilities feel more socially included. Look for work settings where all employees work the same shift. When employees work in different shifts, employees get to know only the people who work in the same shift. Consequently the intimate social atmosphere resulting from everyone working to accomplish the same goal at the same time can be lost.

Consider work settings with an informal management style that encourages team building.

In addition, look for work settings where the employer or supervisor routinely interacts with employees about non-work-related topics. The employer or the supervisor can clearly set the social tone and culture for a work setting; those who are informal in their interactions with employees and promote the concept of teamwork are already practicing inclusive strategies.

Work settings with designated areas for employees to interact socially generally promote social inclusion; the setting indicates that the social aspects of the job are valued.

Social interactions also can be seen as a priority in situations where social activities extend beyond the work setting.

Table 7 summarizes natural support strategies that can be used to help make well-suited and socially inclusive matches between an employee and a job.

Strategies to Modify the Social Environment

Sometimes employees with disabilities can be better included in work settings by making slight environmental modifications to schedules, activities, and routines. Some of these modifications, or natural support strategies, though simple and easy to implement, can be very effective. Relatively unintrusive, they are not likely to disrupt the social culture of the work setting.

Intervention strategies that modify the social environment increase opportunities for employees with disabilities to interact with others. To implement these types of strategies, one must understand the workplace culture, the traditions, routines, and rules, so employees with disabilities can become a part of that culture.

One simple strategy is to assure that the employee with a disability comes to work at the same time as all the other workers. This increases interactive opportunities.

Another strategy—so basic it might be overlooked—is to encourage the employee with a disability to sit or stand more often in specific physical settings where coworkers socialize.

A third strategy is to have the employee become involved in the completion of work tasks that involve other coworkers or supervisors. When employees work together to accomplish a common goal, they tend to interact at natural intervals. Employees may work together side by side, or one employee may be responsible for finishing the first part of task while another employee completes the latter part. To implement this strategy, one must observe work tasks to determine which take more than one person to complete and could include involvement from the employee with the disability.

Let's say the employee with a disability needs to learn a new task at work. Another natural support strategy would have coworkers, rather than the teacher, job coach, or other service provider, teach the task to the employee. In most work settings coworkers assist one another with new work tasks, so this strategy might be a simple extension of the naturally occurring work pattern.

Many work settings have social routines in which all coworkers participate, even though these routines are not listed or specified as a work duty. Such social cultural routines or activities should be identified, to make certain that the employee with the disability participates in them. For example, it may be understood that everyone takes a turn making coffee; if this is the case, the employee with the disability should take a turn making coffee. Perhaps all employees take turns bringing in food to share once a week; the employee with the disability should do so as well. As one might imagine, bring food into a work setting and you usually find conversation around it. People will often comment on the item and will thank the provider. By participating in this type of social routine, the employee with a disability is perceived as being part of the culture.

Of course individuals with disabilities may be reluctant to be a part of these social environmental modifications. Or it may be hard to make these (even slight) modifications in the work setting. If individuals with disabilities do not want to make coffee, that is their choice. If employers want the job coach or teacher, rather than coworkers, to teach employees with disabilities a job task, that is the choice of the employer.

Even with these environmental modifications, there may be little interaction between employees with disabilities and other coworkers. These modifications only create opportunities for interactions; they do not guarantee that interactions will

take place. If interactions still do not take place, it may be that the employee with a disability needs to learn new social skills or that more intrusive natural support strategies need to be tried.

The next section discusses ways coworkers can be involved in interventions to help include employees with disabilities in work settings.

Strategies to Involve Coworkers

Coworkers represent a natural support or resource that exists in all work settings and can facilitate the social inclusion of employees with disabilities. Some strategies require a great deal of coworker involvement; others require only a small amount of effort. Several of these strategies are discussed below.

Initiated by Coworkers

In the ideal natural support strategy, coworkers implement on their own, without any input from the teacher or job coach, a plan or set of procedures that results in the social inclusion of the employee. With this strategy, coworkers socialize with the worker with a disability just as they would socialize with any other worker.

Examples of socialization activities include showing the employee where to store his belongings, training the employee in unfamiliar aspects of the job task, including the employee during breaks and lunchtime, and answering any questions that might come up. These types of natural support strategies involving coworkers generally result in the optimum social inclusion, because they are generated by coworkers and fit most naturally into the culture of the work setting.

The natural support strategy generated and implemented by coworkers can also be used under different circumstances. For example, let's assume that John, an employee with a disability, has trouble accepting negative feedback from his supervisor. When John receives criticism from his supervisor, he scowls and stomps his foot. John's coworkers notice that the only time he is criticized is when he forgets to clean the salt and pepper shakers throughout the day. John's coworkers decide, on their own, to remind John occasionally to clean the salt and pepper shakers so that he will be less likely to be criticized. This intervention works because the coworkers designed something that they could easily implement within the context of their work setting. It also helps John because he receives fewer criticisms from his supervisor.

Suggested by Job Coaches

The ideal social inclusion, natural support strategy, is devised by coworkers. But not all coworkers are able to do this. A second type of strategy relies on the job coach or teacher to suggest interventions to coworkers.

For example, Jane used an augmentative communication system of pointing to pictures to interact with others. Jane's job coach noticed that her coworkers didn't always interact with Jane when she used her book, so her job coach explained the communication system to her coworkers and asked if they would respond to Jane's initiations.

The coworkers agreed to follow this suggestion, admitting that they hadn't been sure at first how to respond when Jane initiated communication with her augmentative system. Clearly the job coach just needed to explain the communication system and make some suggestions to coworkers about how they could interact with Jane.

Instead of making suggestions, job coaches or teachers might solicit ideas from coworkers about the best way to include an employee with disabilities, perhaps by asking several coworkers to a brief meeting before or after work. When the suggestions come from the coworkers, they may be more likely to help out the employee. Also coworkers may have better ideas for supporting inclusion than teachers, job coaches, or other service providers.

Managed by Job Coaches

A possible third strategy requires even more involvement from the teacher or job coach but still enlists the help of coworkers; that is, it requires the teacher to manage the type of support given by coworkers. Here the teacher or job coach identifies the employee's problem and gives specific directions to coworkers about how best to assist the employee.

For example, Stacy often sits by herself during lunch. Her job coach knows that Stacy would like to interact with her coworkers more, so he has a brief meeting in the work setting with two coworkers who seem to be well liked and respected by other coworkers.

The job coach asks the coworkers to sit with Stacy during lunch and requests that they initiate topics of conversation that Stacy enjoys; the coworkers agree that they would also enjoy talking about the topics. In addition, the job coach requests that the coworkers ask Stacy specific questions about particular topics to give Stacy opportunities to talk more (e.g., questions about cooking, which Stacy enjoys). Ultimately the coworkers are involved in the intervention, but the job coach specifies the type of support needed and then provides some instructions on how the support can be implemented.

Taught by Job Coaches

In a fourth type of natural support strategy, coworkers are asked if they are willing to receive training from the job coach or teacher to learn how to engage socially in the work setting with the employee with disabilities. Here teachers or job coaches design the social inclusion intervention and teach coworkers how to implement it.

For example, Joe likes to talk to his coworkers, but he always asks the same questions, over and over again. Joe knows lots of different questions to ask, but he always seems to ask coworkers what they think of the weather and what they had for dinner the night before.

The teacher, who is working with Joe in his vocational placement, asks the coworkers if they would be willing to provide Joe with systematic feedback every time he repeats the same question twice. The coworkers indicate that they are willing to implement the intervention and receive training.

The teacher meets with the coworkers before work and models for them what to say: "Joe, you already asked me that question. Could you please ask me another question?" She also tells the coworkers that if Joe asks a different question, they should continue conversing with him enthusiastically. Then the coworkers practice saying what the teacher has just modeled. The teacher gives feedback to the coworkers and asks to meet with them once a week to see how the intervention is proceeding. In essence, the teacher uses a social skills training package with the coworkers.

In summary, four different types of natural support strategies can be used with coworkers. In some work settings, coworkers will spontaneously design and implement an intervention plan to include the employee and will require little, if any, support from job coaches, teachers, or other service providers. In other work settings, job coaches or teachers may just need to offer a few suggestions to coworkers about what they could do to include an employee, or the job coach or teacher might ask the coworkers for some suggestions about what they think might work best. In a third strategy, the job coach decides the type of support that might be useful and provides some direction to the coworkers about how they could assist with the intervention. With the fourth strategy, the teacher or job coach designs an intervention and trains coworkers to implement the intervention.

CHAPTER FIVE

Changing the Social Skills of Workers With Disabilities

Teach a social skill only if the employee wants to learn the skill and if the lack of the skill is contributing to work problems.

This chapter also describes intervention strategies to facilitate the social inclusion of employees with disabilities. These strategies aim to change the social skills of employees with disabilities.

Three strategies discussed in this chapter can be used to change the social skills of workers with disabilities, principally: (a) social skill training packages, (b) self-directed learning strategies, and (c) cognitive process strategies.

Conditions for Use of Strategies

If two conditions exist, a variety of strategies can be used to change the social skills of workers with disabilities.

Problematic Behaviors

First, the results of the assessment of appropriate social skills should reveal that an employee is having difficulty performing social behaviors needed in the workplace (e.g., asking for help when needed) or is displaying inappropriate social skills (e.g., entering ongoing meetings and talking about a favorite TV show).

These two types of problematic social behaviors (i.e., failing to display needed behaviors or displaying inappropriate behaviors) are of concern if the employee is consequently at risk of losing the job or if assessment results show low acceptance from coworkers. If an employee's assessment results are poor but do not impact her job negatively or affect coworker acceptance, intervention strategies are probably not necessary; there is some degree of tolerance of inappropriate social behaviors in many work settings.

Motivation to Change

Second, before intervention strategies are designed, the employee must want to work on changing her social skills. Social skills are difficult to change, especially for adolescents or young adults. The older people get, the more time they have had to practice and be reinforced for inappropriate or ineffective social skills. This will, no doubt, make new skills more difficult to learn. However, social skills can be changed at any age if the individual is sufficiently motivated.

To meet this second condition, the assessment results in the "feelings and perceptions" category should suggest that the individual with a disability is unhappy with her social situation and would like to do something to improve it.

There are several reasons why employees might want to learn new social skills. First, they might want to improve their skills if they like their jobs but are at risk of losing them because of poor social skills. Second, improved social skills might result in closer social relationships and a greater degree of acceptance from others.

Although these are good reasons to learn new social skills, it is important to tell employees that learning new skills will not guarantee keeping a job or making new friends.

Social Skill Training Packages

When social skills are taught directly using a social skill training package, teachers, job coaches, employment specialists, or other service providers generally take responsibility for the design and delivery of the intervention.

Training Steps

This is a five-step teaching approach, illustrated here using the targeted skill "asking for help."

First, after a particular skill has been identified as a desirable outcome (e.g., asking for help), identify and explain why the employee would want to learn the skill. For example, an employee would want to learn to ask for help if he is at risk of losing a job because he does not request help when it is needed.

Second, describe a social situation at work where the employee would likely ask for help (e.g., "You are trying to install more memory into a computer, and you don't know how to do it"). Then model the social behavior of "asking for help," so the employee could see when to use the skill, and how it looks when others do it (e.g., "When you don't know how to do something like putting memory into a computer, it is important to go up to a coworker or supervisor, look at her, and ask for help, 'Could you help me please?'"). Chapter 3 includes discussion of procedures used to design the social scenarios for role play assessments. It might be useful during this step to ask the employee questions to make sure he understands when help should be requested and how to do it.

The third step is to have the employee practice the skill of asking for help. This step should be practiced several times.

31

The fourth step is to give feedback to the employee about his efforts. This includes providing reinforcing feedback if the skill is done correctly. If the skill is not done correctly, provide corrective feedback (e.g., "Be sure to look at me when you ask for help.").

The last step is to ensure that the employee uses this skill in the actual work setting.

Training Context

If you use a social skill training package, try to teach this skill at a time other than when the employee is working (e.g., during a quick session right before or right after the employee goes to work).

There are two reasons for teaching a skill in off-hours. Teaching the skill while the employee is working might (a) be intrusive and could interrupt work, and (b) call undue and embarrassing attention to the employee. If you teach the skill outside of work hours, the employee can make mistakes and not feel uncomfortable about them.

Generalization

The downside of teaching social skills outside of work hours is the issue of generalization. The employee may always ask for help during the practice sessions but not when she really needs help on the job. To ensure that the social skill generalizes to the work setting, monitor the skill to determine if it is being used. Try to observe directly the employee using the skill or ask coworkers or the employer if the skill has been exhibited. If the skill is not being used, modify the intervention strategy.

> "One of the difficulties associated with teaching social skills is that the tactics learned are not always dynamic; people may be left with a set of behaviors that are not amenable to change or do not adapt to novel, untrained situations."
> —Chadsey & Beyer (2001)

Although there is not enough space in this book to provide an in-depth discussion of generalization, the following teaching strategies promote generalization.

First, try to role play different examples of real situations in which the employee might ask for help on the job. If several examples come from actual work situations, generalization may be enhanced.

Another strategy is to involve coworkers in the instruction, role playing social situations that give the employee an opportunity to ask for help. An intervention that includes coworkers is more realistic than one that includes only the job coach or teacher. Of course coworkers must agree to participate; if the intervention occurs during work, the employer would have to agree to let the coworkers take a break from their duties to participate.

A third strategy is for the teacher or job coach to be at the work site to remind the employee to ask for help when it is needed. For example, the job coach can meet with the employee for a minute or two right before work to remind the employee to ask for help when needed during the work day. This quick reminder might include a mention of a few typical work-day situations for which help should be requested.

During work hours you might also remind the worker to ask for help as the actual need oc-

Table 8

Steps for Using a Social-Skill
Training Package Intervention Strategy

Step	Description
1	Provide a rationale for learning the social skill (e.g., "If you learn this skill, you will be better able to keep your job," or, "If you learn this skill, your coworkers might talk to you more at lunch").
2	Design social scenarios or situations observed at work, and model the social skill for the employee (e.g., you are at work, and you just broke three plates; you go up to your boss and say you are sorry).
3	Have the employee practice the social skill.
4	Provide feedback to the employee on the performance of the skill.
5	Assess for generalization to make sure the employee is using the skill in the actual work setting.

curs. This strategy would require the job coach to know when a real opportunity for asking for help was going to occur. Or you might work with the employer or coworkers to create an on-the-job opportunity when you are onsite to prompt the employee, quickly and quietly, if need be. The risk of using this strategy is that the employee might rely on the job coach to always be around to remind or prompt the skill.

Summary

In summary, a social skill training package requires that a rationale be given to the employee for using the targeted skill. Then the skill should be modeled so the employee can see how it looks and how to do it. Third, the employee should practice performing the skill and receive feedback on the performance. Finally, the person

implementing the intervention needs to ensure that generalization takes place and that the skill is being used in the work setting. The steps for teaching social skills with a social skill training package are included in Table 8.

Self-Directed Learning Strategies

Self-directed learning strategies are used to teach employees to take responsibility for their own social skills, rather than relying on job coaches, teachers, or other service providers. There are several types of self-directed learning strategies, including permanent prompts or cues (e.g., pictures), verbal rehearsal or practice strategies, self-monitoring, and self-reinforcement.

Employees can use these strategies on the job to remind themselves to exhibit appropriate social skills (permanent prompts), to practice these skills (verbal rehearsal), to collect data on their use of the skills (self-monitoring), and to reward themselves if they did a good job using the skill (self-reinforcement). Employees may be taught to use one or a combination of these strategies. As with social skill training packages, instruction would most likely occur during off-work hours. However, once employees learned to use the self-directed learning strategies, they would be expected to use them all the time, especially at work.

Several different strategies are described below, along with examples.

Permanent Prompts

One strategy to consider is to teach employees to use permanent cues or prompts, such as pictures, to remind themselves to use their social skills. The idea behind this strategy is that sometimes we need reminders to do things. Many of us who use lists might also use pictures to remind us of what we must do.

For example, Joe was taught to look at a picture of himself smiling, as a reminder to greet his coworkers with a smile and to say "hello" when he arrived at work in the morning. Right before Joe walked into the building where he worked, he reached into his pocket and looked at a picture of his smiling face. This picture worked as a self-directed learning strategy, because Joe took responsibility for looking at it as a reminder to greet his coworkers.

Verbal Rehearsal

Sometimes it is helpful to practice what we are going to do several times before we actually do it. This is the idea behind another self-directed strat-egy: teaching employees to direct their own social behavior by saying (verbally rehearsing) specific phrases or questions.

For example, Rita was being taught to initiate questions, so she could participate in conversations during lunch and break. Right before she went on break, she would verbally rehearse three questions she could ask by saying to herself, "I could ask, 'How is work going?' or I could ask, 'Did you watch any TV last night?' or I could ask, 'What do think of the weather?' " Rita asked herself these questions several times very quietly before she entered the break room. Of course, Rita had already received instructions from her job coach on when to ask these questions, so she did not ask them at the wrong time during the course of the conversations. Additionally, Rita was taught different questions to ask each week, so she did not always ask the same ones repeatedly.

Self-Monitoring

A third self-directed strategy is self-monitoring. With this strategy, employees are taught to pay attention to their use of social skills and actually collect data about themselves (i.e., whether they performed the skill or not).

For example, Leah was being taught to say "excuse me" every time she had to walk in front of someone, needed to get by someone, or had to interrupt an ongoing conversation. Each time she said "excuse me," she made a click on a golf counter that she carried in the pocket of her apron, which helped Leah to remind herself to be polite and also provided evidence to her (and her job coach) that she was using the polite phrase several times during the day.

Although Leah used a golf counter to self-monitor her social behavior, she could have made a mark on a piece of paper. To make sure she was being accurate about her count, Leah could have also carried a small tape recorder in her pocket to record her examples of saying "excuse me." Then she could have compared the tape recordings to her own count of the times she had performed the social skill. In this way, Leah could have determined how accurate she was at monitoring her social behavior.

Self-Reinforcement

A final self-directed strategy is self-reinforcement or praise. Here employees are taught to praise themselves or give themselves another type of reinforcement after they use the targeted social skill.

For example, Ray's targeted skill was to ask his supervisor every morning what his tasks were for the day. After he asked the question, and his supervisor told him what to do, Ray quietly told himself that he had done a good job.

Summary

In summary, several self-directed learning strategies can be used to teach social skills. Employees can be taught to remind themselves about their social skills through the use of permanent cues or prompts, such as pictures. They also can be taught to self-instruct—to tell themselves verbally what they need to do. To determine if they are performing a targeted social skill, employees can be taught to monitor their own behavior. Finally, employees can be taught to reinforce or praise themselves when they use targeted skills.

Although each of these strategies can be used separately, they can also be combined. For example, employees could be taught to self-monitor their social skills and also reinforce themselves. In addition, these strategies can also be used in combination with social skill training packages.

Overall, the advantage of self-directed learning strategies is that they provide employees with

the opportunity to change their own behavior. With this responsibility, individuals may be more motivated to exhibit appropriate social skills.

Cognitive Process Strategies

As discussed above, self-directed learning strategies can be used to teach social skills either individually or combined in various ways and used as a package. Cognitive process strategies are similar in some respects to self-directed learning strategies, but with cognitive process strategies, employees are taught to use a specific process when they engage in social interactions. This process consists of components that are not used separately; the components are individual steps of a process that a person goes through every time a social situation arises. The process itself is general enough to be applied in any social situation. The strategy is called a cognitive process strategy because most of the steps in the process are internalized (i.e., an individual is taught to think about what he or she needs to do).

Five-Step Process

There are five steps in a cognitive process strategy (see Table 9).

Table 9

Cognitive Process Strategy

1. Establish a social goal.

2. Discriminate or decode specific cues in the social environment.

3. Decide which social skill to use.

4. Perform the social skill.

5. Evaluate or judge the success of using the social skill.

Establish a Social Goal

The first step is to identify the social goal that will be achieved if the social skill is used appropriately. If an employee is not willing to work toward specific social goals, interventions are likely to fail. An employee may want to learn to ask work-related questions, follow directions, or improve conversational skills. The social goal can be generated by the employee or identified through an assessment by the job coach, teacher, or other service provider. Any goal identified through a social skills assessment must be discussed with the employee.

If the employee wants to work on the social goal, the next step in the cognitive process strategy can be taught. But if the employee does not want to work on the goal, it may be best to forget implementing the rest of the intervention. If an employee's job is in jeopardy if certain social skills essential to the job are not changed, you might inform the employee of the possible consequences of not learning the skill; this information might cause the employee to change his mind. Teachers or job coaches can try to teach the skill anyway and hope the intervention is successful. Or you could try to implement some type of natural support strategy (see Chapter 4).

Decode Specific Cues

Let's assume that the employee does want to work on a social goal. The next step in the cognitive process is to teach the employee to discriminate or decode specific cues in the social environment. In this step, the employee must learn to interpret or attach meaning to the verbal and nonverbal behavior of others. She must realize that all social situations are not the same and that only certain social skills are appropriate for certain social situations.

For example, an employee must be able to interpret different nonverbal behaviors, such

as anger and impatience, so that he or she can understand how others might be feeling. The employee also has to understand that the types of social interactions used with supervisors might be different (e.g., more formal) from those used with coworkers (e.g., more informal). An employee also needs to know that the types of social skills exhibited in one part of a work area might be different from those appropriate in another work area. For example, an employee who works in a restaurant may need to use specific social skills out front with customers and different social skills back in the kitchen.

It is apparent that this second step of the cognitive process strategy requires employees to be able to interpret and discriminate among many different social cues. They must understand that different social skills are needed depending upon with whom they are talking (e.g., boss or coworkers), how the person feels (e.g., mad, happy, impatient), where the interaction takes place (e.g., out front with customers or in the back in the kitchen), and when the interaction occurs (e.g., a busy time at work or a slow time at work).

Decide Which Skill to Use

Once employees have learned the second step of the process, it is time to teach the third step of the cognitive process strategy in which employees decide which social skill best meets the requirements of a specific social situation.

This step is very important because there may be several different social skills appropriate for a given social situation. For example, there may be many appropriate ways to ask a coworker a question about what he or she did the night before: "What did you do after work last night?" or "Did you watch any good TV programs last night?" It is also possible that employees may think of asking some questions inappropriate for the situation, for example, "Did you have any sex last night?"

36

If this occurs, it becomes even more essential to teach employees to decide which skills are appropriate and not appropriate for the social situation.

Perform the Skill

The fourth step of the process is to perform the verbal or nonverbal social skill selected. The essential aspect of skill performance is ensuring that when using the skill employees can be clearly understood by others. It does not matter if employees use only one, two, or three words to convey their message, as long as they are understood. It does not matter if employees use augmentative means (e.g., communication books, electronic devices, gestural or sign language) to convey their messages as long as others in the work settings understand the communication. In addition, it is helpful if employees use the right affect (e.g., facial expression) and social distance (e.g., not too close to or too far away from people) when they perform their social skill.

Evaluate Success

In the fifth and final step of the process, employees evaluate or judge the success of their performance. If, after performing their social skills, employees receive positive or neutral responses from others, and if their social goal is met, then they know they've succeeded.

If these two conditions occur (i.e., positive or neutral responses from others and social goal achieved), the employee is apt to use the same process and emit the same social skill in the future when similar social situations arise. However, if employees received negative responses from others or did not meet their social goals, they may need to change their behavior or some aspect of it when they use the cognitive process strategy.

Teaching Example

The cognitive process strategy can be used to teach a variety of social skills. Here is an example of an employee being taught to use the cognitive process strategy of greeting others. Ann works at a health clinic where she does clerical tasks. She is also responsible for carrying patients' charts from one floor of the clinic to another. Ann is a shy person and often does not greet her coworkers.

Ann told her job coach that she wanted to learn to be better at greeting others, so her coworkers would return greetings to her and maybe get to know her better. Ann's job coach knew that Ann had completed the first step of the cognitive process strategy; Ann wants to work on the social goal of greeting her coworkers.

During the next step of the process, Ann's job coach taught Ann when she should and should not greet others. In other words, Ann needed to learn to interpret and discriminate different social situations so she would know when to greet. Ann was taught when to greet (e.g., first thing in the morning and throughout the day as long as 30 minutes had passed since the previous greeting); whom to greet (e.g., coworkers, boss, customers); to recognize how others might be feeling (e.g., don't greet someone who is crying or people who look as if they don't want to be disturbed—if they are working, or if they are in a deep conversation with someone else); and where to greet (e.g., in all areas of the clinic, but not in the restroom if people are inside the bathroom stalls).

Because Step 2 is complicated, Ann's job coach taught Ann to ask and answer the following questions:

1. Whom should I greet?

2. How are these people feeling?

3. When should I greet?

4. Where should I greet?

During the third step of the process, the job coach taught Ann to decide the type of greeting she should use. Ann was taught that she could decide to say "hi," or "hello" or ask "how are you?" Ann was also taught that she should not repeat the greeting if she had already given the same greeting 5 minutes earlier; in this case a smile could be a greeting. Ann was also taught that certain greetings would not be appropriate: not to use the greetings of "hey, what's happening?" and "yo baby." Although these greetings might have been appropriate in some work settings, they were too informal for Ann's medical setting.

In the fourth step, Ann actually practiced her greetings by learning to look at her job coach and say the greeting in a clear, audible voice.

Teaching the fifth step, the job coach reacted either in a positive or negative way to Ann's greeting. Then Ann had to evaluate the success of her greeting based on the response of her job coach.

Ann's job coach taught her this process when she was not working. She told Ann that Ann had to learn to use this process in her head and to do it quickly so that it would become almost automatic.

Because evaluation was part of the cognitive process strategy, each day Ann's job coach asked her to evaluate the success of her greeting skills when she was at work. It took Ann several months to learn the cognitive process strategy, but she became very successful at greeting others.

Summary

Three different strategies can be used to teach social skills to employees with disabilities: (a) the social skills training package, (b) self-directed learning, and (c) cognitive process strategies. How does one decide which strategy to use with a particular employee? There are no specific rules for making decisions about which strategy to use, although several factors should be considered.

The learning abilities of the employee need to be considered when one chooses a strategy; it is best to pick a strategy that is going to be easy for the employee to learn and will likely result in success. For example, the cognitive process strategy requires that the individual must have adequate comprehension and memory skills to learn to use the process. As just described, the cognitive process strategy requires teachers, job coaches, and other service providers to use a lot of verbal language to explain the process. If the employee has difficulty understanding oral language, this strategy may be difficult to teach.

It is also important to choose a strategy that seems to fit best within the work setting. Although many of these strategies may be taught in settings other than the work setting, it is possible that the job coach or teacher may need to teach also onsite, and an overly intrusive strategy may not be appropriate for some work settings.

Whichever strategy is chosen, several issues must always be considered. First, teach a social skill to an employee only if the employee wants to learn the skill and if the lack of the skill is contributing to work problems. Second, if the skill is taught someplace other than the work setting, confirm that it is being used in the work setting.

What Inclusion Strategy to Use?

Sometimes it may make sense to implement both types of intervention strategies; they are not mutually exclusive.

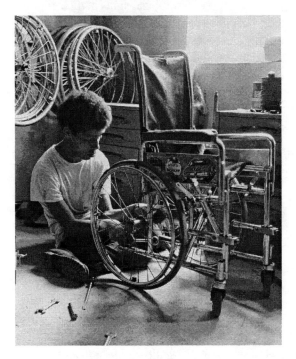

How do you decide which type of social inclusion intervention to use in a work setting? Should you use natural support strategies or social skill training strategies? Although some of these issues have already been discussed, I explore them in greater depth in this chapter.

There has been little research to suggest procedures for choosing the best intervention strategy. After an assessment has been completed, teachers, job coaches, or service providers need to decide if natural support strategies should be implemented, or if the employee with the disability should be taught new social skills. Sometimes it may make sense to implement both types of intervention strategies; they are not mutually exclusive.

First Option: Natural Supports

If the employee with a disability is not socially included in the work setting, first determine if a natural support strategy will work. Natural support strategies should be considered first, because they are least likely to disrupt the work setting and may result in better outcomes than if new social skills are taught.

But the success of natural support strategies depends on the culture of the work setting and the skills of coworkers and their willingness to be involved in intervention efforts. If the culture of the work setting is formal and if coworkers typically don't help each other out, it will be more difficult to implement a natural support strategy. Teachers, job coaches, or service providers will need to assess the work setting to determine the receptivity to natural support strategies.

If natural support strategies are a possibility, the skills and desires of coworkers need to be assessed. Teachers, job coaches, or service providers will have to determine if (a) coworkers are willing and motivated to be involved in interventions, and (b) coworkers have the skills to implement interventions. If coworkers are willing to help out, their level of involvement needs to be determined.

For example, some coworkers may be willing to think of an inclusion plan and implement it on their own with little help from a job coach or teacher. Other coworkers may just want to give feedback to the employee with a disability. Teachers or job coaches may also find that coworkers are willing to be involved in interventions, but they may not have the skills to implement an intervention. If this should be the case, then teachers (or the service provider) will need to teach coworkers the skills for using a natural support strategy.

> In a national study, half of the supervisors and coworkers surveyed did not want to assume sole responsibility for support needs. When they did provide support, many were not as effective in implementing support as were job coaches.
>
> **West, Kregel, Hernandez, & Hock (1997)**

Second Option: Targeting Social Skills

If the work setting is not receptive to natural support strategies, it may be necessary to consider changing the social skills of the employee with a disability. If this approach is taken, there are still issues that need to be considered.

First, if the employee lacks specific social skills, interventions must be designed to teach these skills. The teaching strategy selected must provide the employee with numerous opportunities to practice the skills in environments that will not cause him undue attention or embarrassment. Interventions may vary in intensity and frequency depending upon the skill level of the employee and the complexity of the skills being taught. Because new social skills are not easy to learn, you may need to schedule numerous teaching opportunities.

If employees have social skills in their repertoire but choose not to exhibit them, interventions will need to focus on changing the consequences associated with the lack of performance. Teachers, job coaches, or service providers may need to make certain that the consequences associated with the desired social skill are stronger than the consequences associated with not displaying the skill or performing another competing social skill. For example, if an employee knows how to ask socially appropriate questions (e.g., "What did you watch on TV last night?") but seems to get more attention from coworkers by asking socially inappropriate questions (e.g., "Did you brush your teeth this morning?"), the consequences will have to be changed. One strategy might be to ask coworkers to ignore or respond minimally to inappropriate questions and respond enthusiastically to the appropriate questions.

If employees have the social skills in their repertoires but do not display them fluently, teachers may need to provide opportunities to use the skills more frequently in the work settings. This approach might also enhance generalization, especially if the social skills were taught outside the work environment.

As discussed in Chapter 5, a number of social skills training strategies can be effective, including social skill training packages, self-directed learning, and cognitive-process strategies. If social skill training packages or cognitive-process strategies are used, it is important to ensure that the skills are generalized to the work environment. Self-directed learning strategies may be best suited for performance or fluency problems; they are recommended because they promote active involvement.

Combination Strategies

A combination of strategies may be the most effective. In fact, teachers, job coaches, and service providers may well combine social skill training strategies and natural support strategies. Whichever intervention(s) you select, remember to assess its effectiveness. If the strategy is not working, try another strategy until desired social inclusion outcomes are achieved.

Employee Choice

Finally, when selecting an intervention strategy (whether it is a social skill training or natural support strategy), it is important that employees with disabilities be given responsibility for participating in this selection. You must try to obtain information from employees about which strategies they are most comfortable using and which they think will be most effective. Employees' selection of a strategy will enhance motivation to change.

Additionally employees must be kept informed about the effectiveness of the intervention after it is implemented. As a social inclusion intervention is assessed, employees should receive information about their progress toward achieving their self-selected goals.

For example, assess the feelings and perceptions of the employee to determine if specific outcomes have been achieved (e.g., see if she believes coworkers are now social friends). Or assess the social participation of the employee to see if she is interacting more with coworkers during lunch. Coworkers can also be asked if they socially accept the employee, and individual social skills of the employee can be observed directly during different social activities. The assessment of social outcomes will tell you if interventions are effective in facilitating social inclusion.

Case Study

Thomas used a social skill training package to teach Mara to use the communication book, and he also used natural support strategies by having coworkers ask her questions.

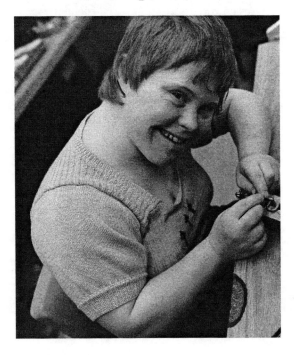

Mara is 17 years old and a senior in high school. Since she was 14, her transition team has worked with her to create a plan by which she could "try out" a variety of jobs in the community. Mara has decided she would like a career in the health and fitness field.

Job Search

During her senior year, her transition specialist, Thomas, was able to get Mara a part-time job at a fitness center. Mara is hoping she will be able to work part time at this job when she graduates from high school. In addition to working part time, Mara is planning to take classes related to health and fitness at the local community college.

As Thomas looked for a job for her, he knew he wanted to find a fitness center with an informal workplace culture and a relaxed pace. He also looked for a manager who seemed to take an interest in the well being of the workers and valued the social aspects of the job.

Although Mara was not a highly social person, she enjoyed talking to others and wanted to work at a job where she might develop some close social relationships. Thomas found a fitness center with a part-time opening that seemed to be a match for both Mara's job and social skills. Although the manager and coworkers had not worked with people with disabilities before, the manager was willing to hire Mara especially because she knew she could depend on the transition specialist to help her out if any problems arose. Mara liked the manager and the job duties, interviewed for the job, and was hired.

On the Job

Thomas worked with the manager and coworkers to teach Mara her job tasks. Mara is responsible for making sure the equipment is clean, organized, and ready for the numerous classes taught in the evenings. In addition, she is responsible for cleaning the weight and aerobic machines after people use them. Finally, she makes certain that there are clean towels available for the customers.

Mara quickly learned the tasks associated with her job, but Mara's transition specialist also wanted to make sure she was being socially included. Through direct observation and informal interviews with coworkers, he determined that Mara was socially participating in activities and accepted by her coworkers. In addition, Mara liked her coworkers and was feeling more comfortable talking to them.

After 2 months on the job, Thomas received a call from the manager. She reported that some of the other workers noticed that Mara had trouble answering some of the questions asked by customers. Mara's speech is not very clear, especially to people who do not know her well. Although Mara tried to answer the customers' questions, she was not making herself understood. These interactions caused the customers to seek out other workers who could answer their questions. These interactions made Mara so frustrated that she started to walk away from all customers when they started to approach her.

The manager said that she and the coworkers were willing to help Mara answer the customers' questions, but they did not know how to make her speech more clear. When they tried to get Mara to imitate what she needed to say, Mara would get upset. Not only was she walking away from the customers, but she was also starting to avoid her coworkers.

Intervention

Thomas met with Mara at school. He reminded her that she needed to advocate for herself and ask others for help if things were not going well on the job. Mara agreed that she should ask for help, but she was embarrassed about her unclear speech.

Thomas asked Mara if she would be interested in using a small communication book as a supplement to her speech. Mara had several of these books that she used in different community settings. The books contained commonly used phrases appropriate for the different places that Mara went. For example, she had a small book for use at the movies, sporting events, and shopping. Mara used these books only when she realized that someone was having trouble understanding her. She would show her book to the person with whom she was talking, point to the phrases and pictures that she was trying to say, and use her speech at the same time.

Mara was willing to have a communication book developed for use at work, although she was embarrassed to have to use something that would make her stand out from others. Thomas asked her if it would be OK to work with her coworkers to get ideas from them on how her book might look; maybe they could think of a way to use the book that would fit in more easily at the fitness center. In addition, Thomas thought that the coworkers might have some good ideas about the type of information that should be contained in the communication book.

Mara and Thomas met with three of her coworkers to develop a plan. Mara's coworkers thought that a communication book would be a good idea. They suggested that Mara keep it in a small appointment calendar that she could carry around with her in her cleaning-supplies basket.

They also worked with Mara to determine the types of questions she was typically asked by customers, including the following questions: Who is the manager? This machine is not working and I can't seem to operate it. Where is the schedule for the classes that are being offered this week? When are the aerobic classes offered? Is childcare available? Can you give me some information about joining this center?

Thomas worked with the speech and language clinician at school to design a communication book that would provide the answers to these questions. Because Mara did not have strong reading skills, a graphic symbol was paired with each answer that corresponded to a question she would likely be asked.

To answer questions not addressed in her book, Mara pointed to a phrase that said, "I don't know, but I will find someone who can help you." Then she would go and get a coworker to help.

Before Mara started her job in the afternoon, Thomas spent 10 minutes with Mara working on her communication book. Thomas pretended he was a customer and asked Mara questions that were answered in the book. Mara was expected to answer the questions within 2 seconds by showing the appointment book to Thomas, pointing to the correct phrase that answered the question, and also verbalizing the answer.

After this brief practice session, Thomas asked Mara's coworkers to come up to Mara at random times throughout her shift and ask the same questions. This gave Mara practice during her working hours. Mara liked to practice with the coworkers; they were nice to her when she was able to answer the questions correctly.

Once Mara could reliably answer all the questions for 3 days in a row, the coworkers were asked to discontinue their "teaching" and interact with Mara as they would with any other coworker.

The coworkers told Thomas that through the brief training, they felt they got to know Mara better and were pleased to help out. One of Mara's coworkers said that she and Mara had some similar interests, and that she was going to ask Mara to go to a movie with her during the weekend.

Assessments

Because the coworkers were no longer going to be involved in the intervention, Thomas asked Mara to use a self-monitoring strategy to collect data on the number of times she was able to answer customers' questions correctly. Mara marked a plus or minus in her appointment calendar each time she was able to correctly (or incorrectly) answer a customer's question.

Several weeks after Mara began to take data on herself, it was clear that Mara had mastered the skill of answering the customers' questions correctly. When Thomas asked Mara how she felt about the using the book, Mara said that she was uncomfortable at first, but then thought it was helpful.

Thomas also asked Mara how she was getting along with her coworkers and if she felt included in activities at work. Mara said she liked her coworkers and had gone out to see a movie with one of them a couple of times. Mara indicated that she was happy at work, looking forward to graduation, and taking classes at the community college so she could learn more about the health and fitness field.

Thomas knew that in order to really understand the big picture of Mara's social inclusion, he needed to ask coworkers how they felt about Mara. The coworkers thought Mara was doing a good job at work and was able to use her communication book effectively with customers.

They also said that she was talking to them more and had come to the latest birthday celebration held for the manager. Conversations with the manager of the fitness center also revealed that Mara was doing a good job. In fact, the manager thought Mara was doing so well that she did not see any reason for the transition specialist to come to work to check up on Mara. She told Thomas that if any problems came up, they would try to help Mara out themselves. If they couldn't, they would give him a call. Thomas was delighted that Mara, her coworkers, and manager had little need for his help.

Summary

Mara's transition specialist used a number of strategies to include her socially on the job. First, he looked for a job in a career area that interested Mara. Second, he looked for a social environment that would be a good match for Mara—one that was informal, social, and was managed by a supervisor who seemed to value the social well-being of employees.

Although Mara quickly learned the job tasks and seemed to get along fine with her coworkers, a problem developed when Mara could not clearly answer customers' questions. Thomas worked with the coworkers and speech and language clinician at school to design a communication book that was part of Mara's appointment calendar. Thomas used a social skill training package to teach Mara to use the book and also used natural support strategies by having coworkers ask her questions throughout her work shift.

In addition, Mara used self-monitoring strategies to keep track of her own performance. When Mara had mastered the use of her book, Thomas assessed her social inclusion by asking about her social participation, workplace acceptance, appropriate social skills, and feelings of social support. When the manager told Thomas that he was no longer needed on a regular basis, he knew that Mara was achieving success.

Conclusions

Social inclusion in work settings is an important outcome for all employees.

Social interactions occur frequently at work; they are important in most work settings for several reasons. If we feel socially included in work settings, we are more likely to be satisfied with our jobs. In addition, work settings are places where we can establish social relationships with others, and social relationships are an important factor in the quality of people's lives. Employees who have good social skills are also more likely to keep their jobs; many employees lose their jobs because they exhibit inappropriate social skills.

It is important to think about jobs that are good matches for a person's job interests and social skills. To feel socially included in work settings, it is helpful for employees to understand the work culture and adjust their social interactions so they fit in. Some work cultures and jobs require highly social workers; others do not.

If we want to know if employees with disabilities are socially included in work settings, we need to assess four areas: social participation, social acceptance by coworkers, feelings and perceptions of the individuals with disabilities, and appropriate social skills. We can make these assessments through strategies including direct observation, sociometrics, rating scales, and role plays.

A number of intervention strategies help facilitate the social inclusion of employees with disabilities. Social inclusion outcomes can be changed through the use of natural support strategies, which can vary from simple interventions (e.g., changing aspects of the work environment so that employees with disabilities have more opportunities to interact with coworkers) to more complex interventions (e.g., teaching coworkers to implement a social skills training program). The best type of natural support strategy involves making a good job match. If a good job match is made, coworkers may include the employee with disabilities in their work culture without needing any help from the job coach, service provider, or teacher.

Social inclusion outcomes can also be facilitated by changing the social skills of the employee. This strategy should be considered only if the employee wants to change his or her social skills and the employee's inappropriate social skills are causing workplace problems. Intervention approaches used to change the social skills of an employee with disabilities include social skill training packages, self-directed learning strategies, and cognitive-process strategies.

Social inclusion in work settings is an important outcome for all employees. The assessment procedures and intervention strategies presented in this book should ensure that social inclusion is a reality for employees with disabilities.

Bibliography

Agran, M., Salzberg, C. L., & Stowitscheck, J. J. (1987). An analysis of the effects of a social skills training program using self-instructions on the acquisition and generalization of two social behaviors in a work setting. *Journal of the Association for Persons With Severe Handicaps*, 12, 131–139.

Argyle, M., & Henderson, M. (1984). The rules of friendship. *Journal of Social and Personal Relationships*, 1, 211–217.

Butterworth, J., Hagner, D., Helm, D. T., & Whelley, T. A. (2000). Workplace culture, social interactions, and supports for transitioning-age young adults. *Mental Retardation*, 38, 342–353.

Chadsey, J., & Beyer, S. (2001). Social relationships in work settings. *Mental Retardation and Developmental Disabilities: Research Reviews*, 1, 122–127.

Chadsey, J. G., Linneman, D., Rusch, F. R., & Cimera, R. E. (1997). The impact of social integration interventions and job coaches in work settings. *Education and Training in Mental Retardation and Developmental Disabilities*, 32, 281–292.

Chadsey, J. G., Sheldon, D. L., DeBardeleben, J., & Cimera, R. (1999). Description of variables impacting successful and unsuccessful cases of social integration involving co-workers. *Journal of Vocational Rehabilitation*, 12, 103–111.

Chadsey-Rusch, J. (1992), Toward defining and measuring social skills in employment settings. *American Journal on Mental Retardation*, 96, 405–418.

Chadsey-Rusch, J., & Gonzalez, P. (1988). Social ecology of the workplace: Employer's perceptions versus direct observation. *Research in Developmental Disabilities*, 9, 229–245.

Chadsey-Rusch, J., Gonzalez, P., Tines, J., & Johnson, J. (1989). Social ecology of the workplace: Contextual variables affecting social interactions of employees with and without mental retardation. *American Journal on Mental Retardation*, 94, 141–151.

Chadsey-Rusch, J., & Heal, L. (1995). Building consensus from transition experts on social integration outcomes and interventions. *Exceptional Children*, 82, 165–187.

Collet-Klingenberg, L., & Chadsey-Rusch, J. (1991). Using a cognitive-process approach to teach social skills. *Education and Training in Mental Retardation*, 26, 258–270.

Greenspan, S., & Schoultz, B. (1981). Why mentally retarded adults lose their jobs: Social competence as a factor in work adjustment. *Applied Research in Mental Retardation*, 2(1), 23–38.

Hagner, D. C. (2000). Coffee breaks and birthday cakes: Evaluating workplace cultures to develop natural supports for employees with disabilities. St. Augustine, FL: Training Resource Network.

Hanley-Maxwell, C., Rusch, F. R., Chadsey-Rusch, J., & Renzaglia, A. (1986). Reported factors contributing to job terminations of individuals with severe disabilities. *Journal of the Association for Persons With Severe Handicaps*, 11(1), 45–52.

Hatch, M. (1993). The dynamics of organizational culture. *Academy of Management Review*, 18, 657–693.

Henderson, M., & Argyle, M. (1986). Informal rules of working relationships. *Journal of Occupational Behavior*, 7, 259–275.

Hinde, R.A. (1995). A suggested structure for a science of relationships. *Personal Relationships*, 2, 1–15.

House, J. S. (1981). Work stress and social support. Redding, MA: Addison-Wesley.

Hughes, C., Hwang, B., Kim, J., Eisenman, L. T., & Killian, D. J. (1995). Quality of life in applied research: A review and analysis of empirical measures. *American Journal on Mental Retardation*, 99, 623–641.

Lee, M., Storey, K., Anderson, J. L., Goetz, L., & Zivolich, S. (1997). The effect of mentoring versus job coach instruction in integration in employment settings. *The Journal for the Association of Persons With Severe Handicaps*, 22, 151–169.

Mank, D., Cioffi, A., & Yovanoff, P. (1997). Analysis of typicalness of supported employment jobs, natural supports, and wage and integration outcomes. *Mental Retardation*, 35, 185–197.

Mank, D., Cioffi, A., & Yovanoff, P. (2000). Direct support in supported employment and its relation to job typicalness, coworker involvement, and employment outcomes. *Mental Retardation*, 38, 506–516.

Ohtake, Y., & Chadsey, J. (1999). Social disclosure among nondisabled coworkers in supported employment settings. *Mental Retardation*, 37, 25–35.

Ohtake, Y., & Chadsey, J. (2001). Continuing to describe the natural support process. *Journal of the Association for Persons With Severe Handicaps*, 26, 84–95.

Park, H. S., & Gaylord-Ross, R. (1989). A problem-solving approach to social skills training in employment settings with mentally retarded youth. *Journal of Applied Behavior Analysis*, 23, 373–380.

Salzberg, C. L., Agran, J., & Lignugaris/Kraft, B. (1986). Behaviors that contribute to entry-level employment: A profile of five jobs. *Applied Research in Mental Retardation*, 7, 299–314.

Stewart, N. (1985). Winning friends at work. New York: Ballantine Books.

Storey, K., & Lengyel, L. (1992). Strategies for increasing interactions in supported employment settings: A review. *Journal of Vocational Rehabilitation*, 2, 46–57.

Wayne, S., & Lidden, R. (1995). Effects of impression management on performance ratings: A longitudinal study. *Academy of Management Journal*, 38, 232–260.

Wehmeyer, M. L. (1998). Student involvement in transition-planning and transition-program implementation. In F. R. Rusch & J. G. Chadsey (Eds.), *Beyond high school: Transition from school to work* (pp. 206–233). Belmont, CA: Wadsworth.

West, M. D., Kregel, J., Herandez, A., & Hock, T. (1997). Everybody's doing it: A national study on the use of natural supports in supported employment. *Focus on Autism and Other Developmental Disabilities*, 12, 175–181.